THIRD EYE AWAKENING FOR BEGINNERS

10 Steps to Activate and Decalcify Your Pineal Gland, Open the Third Eye Chakra, and Increase Mind Power Through Guided Meditation

Kate O' Russell

© **Copyright** 2017 by **Kate O'Russell** - All rights reserved.

The following eBook is reproduced below with the goal of providing information that is as accurate and as reliable as possible. Regardless, purchasing this eBook can be seen as consent to the fact that both the publisher and the author of this book are in no way experts on the topics discussed within, and that any recommendations or suggestions made herein are for entertainment purposes only. Professionals should be consulted as needed before undertaking any of the action endorsed herein.

This declaration is deemed fair and valid by both the American Bar Association and the Committee of Publishers Association and is legally binding throughout the United States.

Furthermore, the transmission, duplication or reproduction of any of the following work, including precise information, will be considered an illegal act, irrespective whether it is done electronically or in print. The legality extends to creating a secondary or tertiary copy of the work or a recorded copy and is only allowed with an express written consent of the Publisher. All additional rights are reserved.

The information in the following pages is broadly considered to be a truthful and accurate account of facts, and as such any inattention, use or misuse of the information in question by the reader will render any resulting actions solely under their purview. There are no scenarios in which the publisher or the original author of this work can be in any fashion deemed liable for any hardship or damages that may befall them after undertaking information described herein.

Additionally, the information found on the following pages is intended for informational purposes only and should thus be considered, universal. As befitting its nature, the information presented is without assurance regarding its continued validity or interim quality. Trademarks that mentioned are done without written consent and can in no way be considered an endorsement from the trademark holder.

TABLE OF CONTENTS

INTRODUCTION 1

CHAPTER 1: *What is the Third Eye?* 2

CHAPTER 2: *Wellness of the Third Eye* 9

CHAPTER 3: *Decalcifying Your Third Eye* 15

CHAPTER 4: *Chakras* 19

CHAPTER 5: *Energy Healing* 26

CHAPTER 6: *Healing Misaligned Chakras* 31

CHAPTER 7: *Mindfulness* 36

CHAPTER 8: *Train Your Brain for Positive Thoughts* 43

CHAPTER 9: *Awaken Your Inner Self with Guided Meditation (1000)* 47

CHAPTER 10: *Awaken Your Intuition* 51

CHAPTER 11: *Reduce Stress with Guided Meditation* 54

CHAPTER 12: *Create a Stronger Brain with Meditation* 58

CHAPTER 13: *5-Minute Guided Meditation* 61

CHAPTER 14: *30-Minute Guided Meditation (1000)* 64

Conclusion 68

INTRODUCTION

Congratulations on downloading your personal copy of *Third Eye Awakening for Beginners: 10 Steps to Activate and Decalcify Your Pineal Gland, Open the Third Eye Chakra, and Increase Mind Power through Guided Meditation.* Thank you for doing so.

The following chapters will discuss the origins of the Third Eye and how it affects every aspect of your daily life. With some soul-searching, it is possible to pinpoint alignment problems within your energy. Doing so allows you to make changes, both physical, mental, and spiritual to change your life.

You will discover how important it is to be fully in tune with your third eye, your spiritual intuition and physical surroundings in your overall wellness.

This book includes two guided meditation sessions that will transcend time and space to align your energies and focus your mind. This tremendous focus allows you to be more functional in daily life, and the ability to connect better with the universe.

There are plenty of books on this subject on the market, thanks again for choosing this one! Every effort was made to ensure it is full of as much useful information as possible. Please enjoy!

CHAPTER 1:
What is the Third Eye?

The third eye is a term reserved for a physical and spiritual part of the body. The pineal gland, in its physical form, is a gland located at the top of the spine that connects with the brain. Physiologically speaking, this endocrine gland has many functional purposes within the body. It is often referred to as the third eye outside of scientific circles. If you were to look someone squarely in the face, the pineal gland would sit just above both eyes, right in the center, like another eye, hence its name.

The pineal gland produces hormones like melatonin and serotonin, which play a big role in regulating sleep patterns and contribute to the overall mood. Without this gland, the body would not recognize normal fluctuations in light, making it difficult to fall and stay asleep in a normal pattern. In the bigger picture, the body would not be able to recognize summer from winter, aside from the change in temperature. The pineal gland exists in most vertebrate animals, and therefore, keep the entire ecosystem running on the same clock, based on sunlight.

While the functional purposes of the pineal gland are generally known, there has always been a bit of mystery surrounding the small gland. Early scientists assumed that this gland was highly important because of its location within the brain. The tiny gland sits dead center between the right and left hemisphere of the brain, and deep under its tissues, almost like the function of the rest of the brain is to protect this small piece. Think of the meat of a walnut encapsulated tightly in its outer shell.

The idea of the pineal gland being a third eye in the spiritual sense is much more powerful than the pineal gland's physical properties. It has long been believed by many cultures that this third eye holds the key to life, and that is no small task. The power of the third eye goes above and beyond recognizing light patterns, and is for channeling energy and light, which is what drives the body.

The power of clairvoyance, seeing the future, is also associated with a strong pineal gland. The idea is that a clairvoyant person has a very strong connection with the universe. This knowledge transcends time and allows you to sense things that will happen in the future. It is not necessarily as depicted on television. A clairvoyant does not necessarily see things happening in the physical sense but through energy.

Many people also see energy in a physical sense. There are auras of energy that surround each and every living thing. The energy emitted takes many different shapes and colors, depending on positive and negative energy. The third eye communicates with the energies of the universe in this way, and learning to recognize these energies is important for ultimate guidance. Many say that negative energy is depicted as red, while positive energies are much lighter, white or shades of green. You would not willingly walk into a room full of people with red auras if you could see them, would you? Likely not, but the average person only sees the room full of people, and enters anyway.

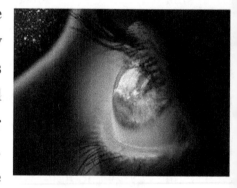

Opening the spiritual eye means seeing the world in a new light, recognizing the connections between your inner energy and that of the universe, and sensing or seeing the energy all around us. Throughout history, the third eye has been celebrated as the utmost in knowledge, education and higher being. Having a well-functioning third eye means having a connection with the higher energy, a God, Gods or any combination thereof depending on classic culture.

We can see the impact of the third eye throughout history in art. Early on, the pinecone became synonymous with the pineal gland. In fact, the name pineal comes from 'pine.' The pinecone had graced this planet with its existence long before any other plant species on earth. It is ancient in nature, and its perfectly aligned spiral structure represents energy and perfection in the deepest senses. Looking through art works throughout the centuries, even dating back to the ancient Egyptians, we see pinecones. It is meant to symbolize divine wisdom and our spiritual soul.

Hindu and Indian cultures also use the pinecone to depict the highest enlightenment and wisdom of their gods. In Hindu culture, all of the gods are depicted in art and lore with pinecones, with Shiva being the most prominent. Indian culture depicts the god Kundalini, with an awakened third eye, bringing wisdom, love, and joy.

The third eye isn't restricted to Eastern cultures, it also spans from Mexico and the Central American region, and even with the Native Americans indigenous to North America. While the traditions and rituals to harness the power of this third eye vary, the outcome is the same. People throughout history have recognized the third eye as the window to their soul, and the connection to their universe.

With all of this discussion of the history of the third eye, it is important to remember that modern man also possesses the pineal gland, the third eye, and a spiritual connection. As time wears on, it seems that humans have become much less connected with their spiritual selves, and the power of the third eye is waning. The importance of spiritual connection often falls by way of modern medicine and factual evidence for what ails us.

What we need to remember is that the spirit is wholly in charge of our physical being and that the energy of the universe is boundless and never-ceasing. We cannot be happy and healthy with a spirit that is unwell. Therefore, it is vital to nurture our third eye and our spiritual connection just as we would treat our bodies well. We need to embrace our spiritual culture and reconnect to be whole, and functional, and human.

If you are looking for science, there is that too. It has been found that the calcification of the pineal gland can be the cause of many physical and mental ailments. This calcification happens when minerals and other elements build up around the gland, causing a decrease in function. Calcification presumes that calcium is the major problem, but other elements, like fluoride and chlorine, also increase the calcification process.

As we age, calcification increases, disrupting sleep patterns and creating overall stress within the body. This stress can manifest itself in a number of ways, including weight gain, chronic disease, and a dysfunctional immune system. Studies have also linked calcification to Alzheimer's disease and memory loss in general.

This gland also produces DMT, a chemical that has been associated with so-called hallucination, and loss of consciousness. This chemical allows us to dream, to enter another world. The idea of this being a hallucination is a fallacy created by man to explain the phenomenon. Those guided by their spirit can recognize that the loss of worldly consciousness and entrance into a higher plane is their soul transcending the body and time as we know it.

Many people have vivid, very real dreams, while others don't. It is believed that the lack of DMT creates a dreamless sleep, and the soul remains stuck within the confines of the body. It is unable to escape and collect wisdom from the universe. Many say they can also find this transcendence through the practice of meditation, a very advanced skill.

These changes in function and behavior can be directly related to a decrease in melatonin DMT and serotonin, but have also long been described in a spiritual sense as losing one's connection with the spiritual universe.

The energy of the universe is all-knowing and helps guide our lives. Being connected helps ensure a steady path in all aspects of life, as the universe gives you the insight and wisdom you need via energy patterns. For example, when you are in a good place, you are surrounded by positive energy, which your body is attracted to. Your third eye has a keen sense of encroaching negative energy, and if you are truly guided by it, can be avoided.

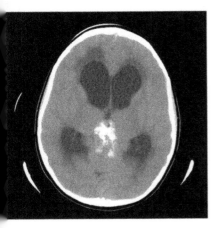

Do you feel connected to the universe? Do you have a keen sense of your surroundings? Do you feel you make good decisions? It is hard to know if the path that you are on is the right one, but there are usually clues. If you feel as if you have no destined path in life, or that you keep making choices that lead you to negativity, you are likely not in touch with your third eye.

This can be a helpless feeling. Imagine that you have cast offshore in a boat with no oars and no sails. The boat aimlessly floats, with no way of steering through deep swells and rogue waves. If this sounds like your life, it is time to reacquaint yourself with your spiritual being. All of the positive energy and wisdom you need lies dormant within you. It is only a matter of harnessing that power to make positive changes in your life.

We can improve this spiritual connection in a number of ways, all of which will be described throughout this book. Learn to decalcify your pineal gland, reconnect with your true self, and with the endless energy of the universe. Your life is special, and you are meant to live a meaningful and productive life. Now is the time to do it.

CHAPTER 2:
Wellness of the Third Eye

As we eluded to in the first chapter, if your pineal gland is out of sorts, problems will manifest themselves throughout the body, mind, and spirit. Paying attention to this tiny gland and keeping it healthy is important to your overall health and wellness. Continuing to neglect, it means new problems will continue to emerge over time.

Physical effects: With modern science taking a hold on our society, let's discuss the scientifically proven, physical effects of a calcified pineal gland, or third eye. Calcium and fluoride are the two biggest calcification culprits, sticking to and creating a hard layer over the gland, decreasing its function. One of the biggest changes will be the output of melatonin, the hormone most well-known for proper sleep and maintaining circadian rhythm.

Other factors can affect the pineal gland as well, including chlorine, environmental chemicals like pesticides, and artificial sweeteners found in an abundance of foods. Basically, any substance that is foreign to the body, and has no way to manage can affect the pineal gland.

The direct effect will cause trouble falling and staying asleep, especially compared to your normal pattern. A good indication of calcification is an

melatonin

abrupt change in your normal sleeping pattern that cannot otherwise be explained. Keep in mind that increases in stress, caffeine too close to bedtime and a poor sleeping environment can all contribute to this problem.

Melatonin is also responsible for a number of other functions, including proper onset of puberty in children. If the pineal gland is affected by excess fluoride in the diet, delayed puberty can occur, which will affect the course of growth and reproduction. In adulthood, a calcified pineal gland can also spell trouble for conceiving a child and overall sexual capabilities. Problems with sex drive and fertility have clear links to decreased melatonin caused by a dysfunctional pineal gland.

Melatonin is also an integral part of the body's natural defense against free radical damage. Simply put, free radical damage occurs when cells are exposed to environmental toxins, oxidation, and stress. These factors stress and cause damage to cells, leading to cell death. This break-down of cells means that your overall function decreases, and the aging process quickens. Melatonin is on the front lines of helping cells battle free radicals and conserve healthy cells.

If you are feeling generally sluggish and tired, even with adequate rest, there is a good chance your pineal gland is calcified, and this process has already begun. Depression is also another common symptom, as serotonin, your 'happy hormone' is greatly affected as well. While depression can be situational, if you are feeling low most of the time and nothing seems to help your depression, it could point to your pineal gland as the culprit.

Emerging science has also shown that the pineal gland has ties to cancer, hypertension and other chronic diseases that were once thought to be independent of each other. As research continues, we find that all systems within the body are connected, and hormonal imbalances, much like the one happening in a calcified pineal gland can be the true root causes of chronic disease.

Perhaps one of the most interesting developments from a calcified pineal gland is excessive cravings for alcohol. While the cause is still being explored, it is well documented that calcification and alcoholism correlate with each other. This implies that pineal gland calcification can actually be a root cause of alcoholism, and can certainly hinder the treatment process.

Emotional effects: As we touched upon earlier, a dysfunctional pineal gland can have a major impact on emotional health. There is some fascinating science out there explaining how environmental factors like magnetic fields and toxins can alter our mental function through our pineal gland.

As we discussed earlier, the pineal gland is not exclusive to humans, it is found in all vertebrate animals. In other mammals, the gland functions as a compass, something that orients the animal in time and space. It works off of positive and negative energy, magnetics associated with the earth's atmosphere. For example, birds know where and when to fly south for the winter because of changes in light (melatonin), and by following the magnetic pathways of the earth. Studies have shown that changing the magnetic field around the bird will cause disorientation.

This is a fascinating fact because it can be applied so easily to humans. We would be foolish to think that the same gland birds have is not functioning the same way in humans. Perhaps this is why centuries of culture have named the pineal gland the source of knowledge, wisdom, and guidance. This gland is literally responsible for our orientation within the world, both in the physical and emotional sense.

Further studies insist that changes in electromagnetic fields, like that occurring during a solar flare, actually increases the incidence of depression and suicide in humans. The vast changes in magnetics disorient the pineal gland, causing decreases in melatonin and serotonin, increasing depression.

While changes in magnetics can be a supporting factor, it is well known that environmental effects of improper diet, chemical exposure, and environmental toxins are more likely causes of pineal trouble. Long-term exposure to any number of these elements cause calcification, and suppressed hormones, specifically serotonin.

As we know, suppressed mental and emotional capacity affects the outcomes of life. When we are tired, from lack of restful sleep, we are short-tempered and ineffective. It will hinder our ability to work, creating stress within our jobs. Concentration wanes with lack of sleep, making even the simplest tasks most difficult.

When you are tired, it seems the only thing to think about is getting to sleep, making it through the day, scraping by, waiting for your head to hit the pillow. Once it does, the illusion of sleep may appear, but actually doing so may not be possible. Melatonin has not been produced, and therefore, you are struck with insomnia. This cycle of fatigue and insomnia is caused by this imbalance, and over time, can be debilitating, and downright maddening.

It is really no wonder that with our hectic work schedules, exposure to heavy metals and toxins, poor diets, any of us are even alive. Many of us muddle through life, hoping to feel better someday,  yet stuck in a depression that keeps us from even having the energy to try to make positive changes. This is depression and poor mental health.

Spiritually

Followed directly behind our emotional demise is our spiritual one. The third eye is seen as our pathway to seeing the world and the universe around us. Energy naturally flows in and out of it, guiding us and bringing joy and light to our lives. It is the pathway for our inner selves, our souls, to shine through. A calcified pineal gland forms a shell around our third eye, hindering its ability to see, and to be everything it needs to be.

Our spirit can easily become suppressed, buried away within that shell, making it nearly impossible to live our best lives. Imagine that your inner self at its best creates a huge aura around you that shines bright, attracting and grabbing positive energy and guiding you forward. Imagine its suppression as that bright light being just a small ember, tucked away inside your mind. On the outside, your spirit doesn't show, and you wander aimlessly hoping for direction.

Most of us know from experience that feeling depressed or tired really hinders the spirit. It is very hard to feel enlightened, free and boundless when we barely have enough energy to get through the day. There is no room for creative ideas, big dreams, and there is certainly no drive to go after it without a true spiritual backing.

There is no doubt that a calcified pineal gland will affect your overall quality of life. Now that you have seen the different possible side effects of a dysfunctional third eye, it is time to take steps to fix it. Continue to the following chapter for ways to eliminate environmental toxins, fluoride and the like. You will be glad you did!

CHAPTER 3:
Decalcifying Your Third Eye

In the last chapter, we determined that a number of factors can cause calcification of the pineal gland, your third eye. The result is a host of physical, emotional and spiritual symptoms that really hinder the way you live your life. Taking steps to decalcify your pineal gland can improve these symptoms and quicken your path to enlightenment.

There are a number of lifestyle changes that can be made. Two of the major causes of calcification are fluoride and chlorine. Both of these elements are found in nature in trace amounts. The likelihood of coming across these on a regular basis would be pretty slim, except we are now using them in things like drinking water and swimming pools. Our exposure is greatly increased and causes calcification.

Fluoride is often found in city water systems. It is a necessary element in the diet and has been found to prevent dental issues. It is added to tap water to make sure we are getting enough. But is it too much for our pineal glands? Using a private well, if possible, is the best way to get your drinking water in regards to fluoride. Keep in mind that other heavy metals may exist if there is a lot of iron or magnesium in your soil. Another option is using a water filter that removes fluoride and other metals.

Most of us are not swimming in a chlorinated pool daily, so it is not much of a concern. What is of concern is a mineral we have all been told is good for us in abundance: calcium. This mineral makes up our bone structure and is necessary for chemical reactions and nerve function throughout the body. While an abundant supply is great for these things, the excess will calcify in places like the kidneys and pineal gland, causing problems.

An easy way to make sure you are getting enough calcium without the excess is to take in adequate Vitamin D. This vitamin helps transport excess calcium to bones, or to the kidneys to be voided from the body, instead of building up around the pineal gland.

We also need to look at other heavy metals, like aluminum as a possible cause of calcification. Like calcium, an excess of heavy metals like aluminum and iron can cause a problem as well. Iron is often found in drinking water and in a number of foods. Excess iron can cause slowing of the gastric system, causing constipation.

Aluminum is found in many personal hygiene products, like deodorant. Most people use this daily, constantly exposing themselves to a metal that could be causing them harm. Aside from the pineal gland, high amounts of aluminum have also been shown to interfere with a variety of hormones, including melatonin.

Food: While a number of these heavy metals and pollutants are unavoidable due to our surroundings, the food you put in your body is something completely under control. Research has shown that artificial dyes, sweeteners, and chemicals not otherwise found in nature can cause calcification of the pineal gland as well. Processed foods often contain preservatives to extend shelf life, and to improve the taste or texture of the product.

The human body has not evolved as quickly as our modern food system, and so does not recognize these new compounds as something it can process. The majority of it gets excreted from the body, but a good deal circulates in the blood and collects in areas, like around the pineal gland, affecting chemical reactions in cells.

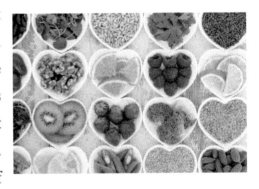

Eliminating foods that contain foreign substances and replacing them with whole foods that the body recognizes is a great way to start recovering your pineal gland. Reducing the number of agents that are bombarding the gland will help reverse the process.

In addition, adding in foods that contain antioxidant properties help the process of detoxification and decalcification along. Be sure to include a variety of fruits and vegetables, nuts, and seeds. This combination of Vitamin E, C and D foods stimulates the immune system and fights free radicals.

There is a great deal of information and advice for decalcification, including taking melatonin supplements to help regulate the system. While supplementing may help your circadian rhythm get back in check, the body adjusts to this addition, and slows melatonin production by the pineal gland, as it just isn't necessary. Supplement for the short term to get the rest you need, but it is not recommended to maintain supplementation long term.

Anecdotal evidence can support sunlight therapy for stimulating melatonin production as well. Since calcification hinders the pineal gland from 'seeing' light, adding more light seems to stimulate the process. In turn, making sure to sleep in completely dark spaces creates a definite positive (sun) and negative (darkness) to redevelop the circadian rhythm.

Another important part of this process is reducing stress. Environmental stress, like a hectic schedule and strained relationships, play a large role in calcification of the pineal gland. Letting go of some responsibilities, and practicing yoga and meditation are a great way to de-stress. Take time to care for yourself so that you may live as you should.

CHAPTER 4:
Chakras

Another aspect of spiritual awakening is recognizing and working with the chakra system. Chakras are centers where energy collects throughout the body. They are generally centered around major organ systems, and manipulating the energy and clearing blockages of energy in these areas can help bring more balance to your life and alleviate symptoms associated with a specific chakra.

The chakra system was originally developed in India, centuries ago, and it still plays a major role in Eastern medicine today. Chakras are all about energy balance. Just like your spine, the alignment of your chakras must be just right, or there will be a pain. Learning to pinpoint when a chakra point is out of alignment is the key to fixing it. The body and mind are in a constant state of finding balance. Energy flows and changes, and it is necessary to take stock of your needs, both physical and emotional, as it relates to your chakras, on the regular.

There are seven major chakras in total, all aligned along the center line of the body. They are as follows:

Root Chakra: This energy point is located at the base of the spine, at the tailbone. It is called the root chakra because it is meant to be the energy that grounds you. As you sit on the floor, this chakra is directly in line with the energy of the earth, literally grounding you to it. On a spiritual level, this energy is what keeps you humble and centered in everyday life. It is what gives you purpose, and continually reminds you of your purpose.

A misaligned root chakra can have you feeling as if you are not grounded, unstable. It can manifest itself as having money issues, insecurity finding housing, or a place to call your own. Energy imbalance in this area may lead to trouble securing food or feeling as if you are satisfied. It is associated with the color red.

Imbalance may manifest itself as stiffness in the legs, knee issues, sciatica, a weak immune system, and eating disorders.

Sacral Chakra: This chakra gives us the ability to interact and accept others. It is the energy that drives exploration and new experiences. It is located just above the root chakra, about two inches below the navel. Energy from this chakra drives passion and sexual desire, pleasure, and abundance.

A disrupted flow of energy in this chakra can cause a decrease in sex drive, little ability to connect with others on an emotional level and show interest or desire in anything. This chakra is commonly associated with the symptoms of malaise and disinterest during depression. Lack of energy here makes it difficult to show compassion for others and find common ground. It also makes you less able to accept inevitable change in life.

Lack of energy here can manifest itself physically as urinary or sexual issues, kidney problems, and lower back pain.

Solar Plexus Chakra: This concentration of energy is centered in the upper abdomen, near the stomach. It is the driving force for our self-confidence and self-esteem. Without this energy, we do not have the courage to follow through with our goals and aspirations. Without it, we are meek and have no confidence in our capability of success.

Like our pineal gland, the solar plexus helps guide and drive life forward. You may recognize its power as that itch to do something new, to try new things and become more successful. This power waxes and wanes as the chakra moves in and out of alignment. It is associated with the color yellow.

Energy drops may manifest with general fatigue, digestive issues, gallbladder or pancreas issues, including diabetes.

Heart Chakra: It's no surprise that this mass of energy is located on the spine right next to the heart. It is responsible for joy, love and peace. Our heart organ often gets the credit for love, but it is really a beaming ray of

energy from our heart chakra that fills our chest cavity with feelings of excitement and warmth.

Strengthening this chakra increases our ability and capacity to love, and at what magnitude. It defines the relationships we have and keep. It is associated with the color green, not red, as you might expect!

Issues with respiratory infections, asthma, heart disease and circulatory issues can be a physical manifestation of low energy in the heart chakra.

Throat Chakra: This little gem is centered right in the center of our throat. It is responsible for our ability for good communication. When in good alignment, this chakra gives us the energy to articulate our ideas and needs in a way that others can easily understand.

When out of alignment, it may be difficult to work with others and get your point across. We all have moments when it seems like no matter how well you explain something, people don't understand you. Not enough energy is available to formulate your words and emotions in such a way that makes an impact on others.

Issues with the thyroid, laryngitis, ear infections, and shoulder or neck pain are a good indicator that your throat chakra is out of alignment.

Third Eye Chakra: Yes, it has its own chakra! It is really no wonder that a great mass of energy is centered right where the third eye is located, just above the eyes in the center of your forehead. As we have discussed, this chakra is responsible for your intuition and decision-making skills.

You may have felt a decrease in this chakra's energy before, manifested as an inability to make a decision. Generally, wishy-washy people lack energy in this chakra, as their inner self is unable to guide their decisions, leaving them hanging, wondering what to do. Realigning this chakra invites wisdom and confidence that you are making educated decisions.

Chronic headaches, blurry vision, and hormonal imbalance, can all be signs of a third eye energy deficiency. We also cannot forget about depression and anxiety as possible symptoms.

Crown Chakra: Last, but not least, the crown chakra represents our ability to be connected spiritually. It is located at the very top of the skull. It represents our ability to see beauty in the world and have joy within us. As you sit in a seated position, you are rooted in your root chakra, and your spine stands lengthened with your crown chakra pointed straight up to the heavens.

In meditation, this chakra will attract and accept energy in through your head and radiate all throughout your body. Lacking energy in this area means you will find little joy in your surroundings and the rest of your chakras will suffer from lack of energy as well.

Sensitivity to light and sound, as well as depression and the inability to concentrate or learn, are good indications of a problem with your crown chakra.

Knowing the spiritual functions of each chakra makes it easier to pinpoint when any one is out of alignment. Our bodies and spirits are in a constant state of fluctuation, so at any given time, any chakra may not be functioning properly, even on a day to day basis. It is important to recognize these subtle changes so that adjustments can be made to realign the energy balance.

If one chakra is out of alignment for a long period of time, it begins to really show. For example, if your root chakra is out of whack, you may notice that you lose your ability to control spending, pay bills and keep a secure home. There just isn't enough energy to focus on these things. Over time, the problems mount, creating stress. Aligning this chakra at subtle hints of a problem can help avoid things like financial ruin, loss of relationships or declines in health.

The imbalance of one chakra also causes the overcompensation of others, in effort to try and balance themselves. This can manifest in a number of ways, depending on which is acting up. You may be doing very well in one aspect of life, but completely failing in another, something many of us recognize. The goal is to balance all energies, so we are strong and successful in all areas of life.

CHAPTER 5:
Energy Healing

Managing your inner energy requires a bit of maintenance, just as with choosing a healthy diet. The activities you choose to do, both physical and mental, play a role in the health of your inner energy, or your Chi, as it is called in Eastern medicine. Energy healing does not require a lot of money or time, but it does require some effort and, for beginners, guidance from an experienced healer.

Let us begin with the simplest method of all: energy transfer. This is simply manipulating the energy around your body to get it flowing. Energy naturally flows in a circular pattern throughout your body but can get blocked, building up in some places, and starving others. Think of this energy as your blood, coursing through your veins. A blockage can cause catastrophic problems within the system if it cannot be unblocked.

Energy transfer is a simple thing you can do every day to keep your energy flowing, and it is a great technique to add to your meditation practice. It is possible to move energy through your body by thought and gentle touch. The key is to recognize where this blockage may be occurring, so you can pinpoint that area. This may be a physical symptom, like pain in your shoulders, or a stomach ache. Simply sit still, place your hands gently over the afflicted area.

For example, if your stomach is upset, place your hands gently on your belly. Imagine that energy from all over your body is collecting in your hands, almost to the point where they tingle. Next, think about that energy flowing from your hands, into your belly, and washing it with health.

It will take a bit of practice to feel the effects of this technique. It takes a good deal of concentration to harness that energy and redistribute it properly. If you are new to meditation and energy work, seek the help of a professional. It is possible to do energy work on another person and to feel the effects, you may need to harness energy from another.

A professional Reiki practitioner will be able to help you determine where your energy needs improvement and can help open the lines of spiritual communication again. Reiki is open and beneficial to everyone, including those who may be skeptical of its benefit. Energy does not care about skepticism and will work regardless of belief.

Reiki is not a religion, and therefore, is truly open to everyone. You do not need to subscribe to any religious aspects of practice, making it more of an open field, much like massage therapy or acupuncture.

Whenever you are working with a practitioner in such a personal way, it is important to trust and feel comfortable around this person. There are people you may not click with, and others you do. If your first Reiki session doesn't seem quite right, don't give up. Give the benefit of the doubt and try again, or find another practitioner.

Acupuncture is another great way to remove energy blocks and get it flowing again. This ancient practice originated in China around 6000BC. Instead of needles, practitioners used sharpened animal bones to target a number of pressure points around the body.

Adding pressure and a skin prick to an area of concern causes the body to send blood flow and energy to that area for healing. This flood of energy unblocks the system, and the symptoms can be relieved. Acupuncture can be used to treat just about any ailment, from physical pain to emotional trouble.

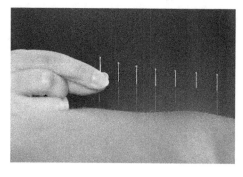

Because acupuncture requires a sanitary, sterile environment, it is recommended to only receive acupuncture from a licensed professional. Find someone who is licensed by your local health district and who has a proper education. It is possible to transmit diseases via these needles, so a practitioner who follows the rules and disposes of used needles is of utmost importance.

Moving your body is another great way to get that energy flowing. We have known the correlation between general exercise and good health for quite some time. We often associate a healthy person as one who moves their body regularly. Starting or improving upon an existing exercise regimen can certainly improve the flow of energy and overall health.

Not all exercise is created equal. Many people make the mistake of exercising certain parts of the body and not others. For example, a walker may work their legs and heart, but their upper body is largely unchallenged. A bodybuilder may focus on muscles but not cardiovascular strength. The majority of people focus too much on the exercise itself, and not the stretching.

In addition, exercise is usually not done with optimal energy flow in mind. People focus on the task, but not the purpose, when really, the idea is to create an open channel of energy flow, getting oxygen and blood to all areas of the body, including vital organs. There are some exercises that are better than others at this.

Yoga is a wonderful practice that has been catching steam in the exercise world in the last decade. There are many different versions and classes available, with different ideas for what is right. Really, none of them are wrong, just different. Some classes focus on the same set of poses, while others change the routine often, even others that focus mostly on meditation.

Find a method that speaks to you by trying different versions, and figuring out what makes you feel your best. The immediate effects of yoga are clear. Those who practice report feelings of euphoria and lightness within their bodies directly after practice, and for the rest of the day in most cases. The practice relieves stress, stretches your muscles and moves energy around.

Practicing yoga does require basic physical strength and capability but is also something that improves with practice. If you are in good health in general and able to move, it is a great option. If your mobility is limited, it is possible to modify poses as well.

Qui Gong and Tai Chi are both ancient practices that focus on the flow of energy. If you were to watch someone practicing either one, it might remind you of karate or other martial arts, but at a much slower pace. The hand and leg movements mimic traditional moves but in a constantly-flowing slow-motion way. It is really quite a sight, and the benefits of stress relief and physical exercise associated with this practice enhances energy flow.

No matter what type of energy healing you subscribe to, regular participation in something that helps keep your energies balanced is a must in this stressful world. Your energy can take a shift in one direction or another at a moment's notice. It is important to recognize this and make adjustments as necessary so that you may live your best life.

CHAPTER 6:
Healing Misaligned Chakras

Healing misaligned chakras means knowing which ones need work. If you haven't already, check out the chapter on chakras, and each of their responsibilities. This is your guide for figuring out where your energy may be blocked so that you can make the best effort to fix it.

First, how do you know your chakras are blocked? You may feel easily overwhelmed, stressed and anxious. Instead, you may feel depressed and disinterested in anything and everything. Making even simple decisions may seem difficult, and you may feel like you are wandering aimlessly, looking for something to spark your interest.

Since our chakras are our guiding centers in the body, it makes sense to feel a little lost and aimless, as we are left to our own devices to make good choices and decisions. When our chakras are aligned, we can see the path more clearly, making us more confident in our decision making. It is important to note that this feeling is inevitable in all of our lives, but we can certainly reduce their effects. So let's get them back in order, shall we?

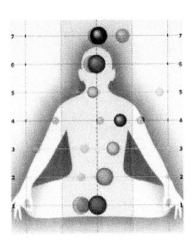

Let us explore ways to heal each individual chakra:

Root Chakra: keep in mind that this chakra roots you to all of your moral values and worth. Having a weak root chakra may be associated with feelings of inadequacy when it comes to money, or making good decisions. Physical manifestations include problems with general fatigue and leg problems, including arthritis.

Using essential oils like cedarwood or myrrh for aromatherapy can help align your roots. Deep scents like clove in your cooking help ground your energy. In yoga, focus on poses that keep your feet grounded to the floor. Make sure all four points of your feet are solidly rooted to the ground.

Sacral Chakra: Remember that the sacral chakra is what drives passion, desire and emotion. If you are feeling a bit withdrawn from people, feel little desire to be friendly or are not relating to basic emotions, this chakra is likely out of alignment. Physically, you may be having problems with fertility and sexual performance, among other things.

Use aromatherapy with jasmine to help bring new life into this chakra. When it comes to exercise, abdominal-strengthening exercises and yoga poses help bring strength to that area. In yoga, warrior poses and those that generate heat (challenging poses) will strengthen your sacral chakra.

Solar Plexus Chakra: A lack of energy in this chakra can lead to anxiety and digestive issues.

While having an overall healthy diet is a must, eating foods with ginger and lemon tend to be particularly soothing. Try starting your day with a mix of ginger and lemon tea. Aromatherapy with essential oils like lemongrass or rosemary applied to your wrists will get that energy flowing as 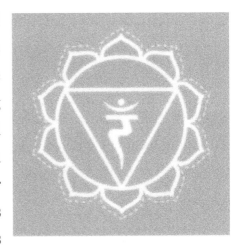 well. Focus on back-bending yoga poses like sun salutation, bow, and twists.

Heart Chakra: Located at the center of your body near the heart, this chakra is responsible for feelings of love and joy. A lack of energy in this chakra may manifest as loneliness and disconnection. It greatly affects your ability to love and the capacity at which you do so. Physically, it may manifest as respiratory issues like chronic bronchitis, heart trouble, and blood circulation problems.

It is vital that you keep this chakra balanced. Using essential oils like rose early in the morning wake up this chakra. Cooking with herbs like thyme also help. When it comes to yoga, focus on chest-opening exercises like cobra. Breathing deeply and mindfully also help breathe new life "literally" into your affected lungs.

Throat Chakra: Having a healthy throat chakra means that you can effectively communicate with people. If you are feeling as though you are not being heard, or that you are often misunderstood, this could be the problem. In addition, having issues with your thyroid or respiratory system, this could be the culprit.

To bring energy to this chakra, use eucalyptus oils. We see this oil commonly used in chest rubs to open up airways during sickness, and this is basically the same concept. Opening up your neck and shoulders with head and neck rolls keep the area loose and functional.

Third eye chakra: If your intuition escapes you and you feel a bit misguided, it's time to focus on your third eye chakra. There is no doubt that meditation will certainly help open your inner spirit via your third eye.

In addition, essential oils like sage, jasmine, and mint help awaken your senses. Cooking with mint, sage or bay leaves helps too. In yoga, child's pose helps you draw into yourself, putting your forehead to the ground to accept the energy of the earth.

Crown chakra: Feeling a spiritual connection has a lot to do with your crown chakra. Your true happiness may be feeling a little low or may be having some nerve issues associated with a lack of energy here.

While oils with floral scents and sandalwood help, meditation and activity are really the best ways to energize this chakra. Yoga poses that require great balance, like Tree, help focus your energy. Being outdoors helps you feel more connected to the bigger picture as well. Get outside for a walk every day.

If you are not sure which chakras are out of alignment, try doing a little of each of these things on a daily basis. Meditation, in general, will help bring energy and awareness to your body, as well as reconnect your mind with your inner self. Practice daily using different techniques to reap the most benefit.

Use a combination of essential oils throughout the week to heighten different senses and get your energy flowing. Get outside and connect with nature and get some much-needed physical activity in the process. If you practice yoga, do a good variety of poses that meet the needs of all your chakras.

CHAPTER 7:
Mindfulness

Perhaps the easiest way to quicken your path to enlightenment is with mindfulness. This buzzword has caught the attention of those seeking for better mental health and connection recently. The idea is very simple. In short, being mindful is about being present in your life, and really engaging in it.

The best example of living mindlessly is driving. How many times have you gotten in the car, buckled your seatbelt, and came to when you arrived at your destination. No, you didn't fall asleep, but your mind did wander away from the task at hand. Not only is this a bit dangerous as your attention is split, but it means that you have missed out on the sights and sounds of the journey, missed a cute dog with its head out the window, a cluster of birds flying in unison instead. What did you trade this for? Another moment worrying about something deep in your own head?

The biggest risk you take with mindlessness is missing out on the little things in life that bring you joy and excitement. These small things are often overlooked, and doing so leads to a life of boredom, little stimulation and a wish for something

more.

At this point in life, you may have backed yourself into a corner spiritually. Feelings of inadequacy, stagnancy, and hopelessness are common, and can all be tied back to your spiritual health. Had you been in touch with the needs of your inner self, you may have realized sooner that the life you live is not what excites your soul. What can we do about it?

Practicing mindfulness is a great way to reconnect with your inner self. It helps you get in tune with your deepest needs and desires in a way that is tangible and impossible to ignore. Once you are aware of exactly what you want, you will have no choice but to follow a path that will lead you to it. This awakening is a total shift in your soul and way of life. Why wouldn't you want that?

So start practicing mindfulness today. Getting started is very easy. It requires no other tools than the power of your mind. Here are some tips to get going:

Pay attention: The idea of multi-tasking has often been touted as a great resume booster, but dividing the focus of the mind means you are using less brain power for each task you juggle. Instead, focus wholeheartedly on whatever it is you are doing.

Are you enjoying the task? Does it fulfill you? Are you at least doing it right? Practice with small things, like washing dishes or folding laundry. Ordinarily, your mind might wander. Instead, focus on scrubbing each dish, folding each shirt.

The added benefit of this exercise is stress relief. If you are focusing all of your attention on one thing, it is impossible to stress about another. Take the time to relax your stressed brain and just do something simple. There will be plenty of time to focus on your problem once the laundry is done. Relaxing your brain gives it the capability to push more energy toward fixing the problem later on.

Feel the energy: Ever get stuck in a stressful situation, one where you could taste the tension? Even the dullest of pineal glands can sense when the energy in a room is very off. It takes a little more attention and finesse to sense the small fluctuations. These are subtle hints that things are well....or not. Pay more attention to exactly how you are feeling in different situations. You will notice certain situations have you relaxed and calm, while others make you afraid and stressed. Be able to distinguish between feeling stressed and excited.

Feelings are the body's way of telling you something is off. Instead of pushing those feelings away or writing yourself or others off as being too emotional, listen and feel what is going on. This is your inner self-warning you that you are off track. You would be wise to take a step back and figure out what isn't quite right before moving forward. Don't worry, when things are good, you will recognize it!

People: Everyone has their circle of friends. Some are very close, some on the outskirts. Naturally, there will people who are drawn to you and vice versa, but others who you are repelled by. While we usually blame this on things like personality and values, it really comes down to the energy you give off. Instead of basing relationships and interactions on words and actions alone, listen to your inner self and take this as advice if something feels a little off.

Job: Each and every one of us has once had a job that they hated. For whatever reason, the atmosphere, the people and the work, in general, were not very satisfying. Our spirits are driven by challenges, and overcoming obstacles and celebrating that victory is in our very nature. Jobs that are stagnant and repetitive are a recipe for spirit burnout. There is nothing intriguing or new about it, and we lose interest very quickly.

Unfortunately, in life, people need to work in grocery stores, input data in computers and the like. Some have more affinity for it than others, but if you feel stuck in such a position, you do have options. Ideally, you will find a better position for yourself. Moving up to a managerial position where you have more creativity and flexibility will fuel your innermost desires. Maybe you forgo a formal job and become an entrepreneur, totally feeding the flame.

Sometimes, these options are not available, at least not right away. If you are looking to improve your happiness and well-being today, quitting your job isn't on the list. In fact, moving quickly without a plan can cause more stress than it relieves. Instead, find the little joys of every day. Reconnect  with co-workers, find the pleasant parts of your job and savor them. If you can't find the silver lining, at least make sure you are doing something of value in your off hours. Do things that bring you happiness and peace after work or on your days off to help carry your spirit through work.

The funny thing is, the universal flow of energy becomes a little off kilter when you aren't at your best. To relieve that imbalance, positive energy flows your way. If you are willing to accept it, your energies can be balanced, and you will be back in a good flow. Most people are closed off to the idea of taking help, whether it be in the form of positive energy, or with a leg up from a friend.

There are often very blatant signs pointing you in the direction of a way out, but we are too stubborn, thick-headed and blind to recognize it for what it is. This is where mindfulness kicks in. If you are aware of your surroundings, can feel the energy flowing around you, and be open-minded enough to take an opportunity once it presents itself, your life can move forward.

Practicing mindfulness is just that; practice. You cannot expect to be fully enlightened in one afternoon of mindful thinking. It takes consistent effort and practice to create awareness and attract positive energy to yourself. Take some time each day to take stock of your emotional and spiritual well-being. Think about how the events of the day affected your mood and your energy levels.

Think of it as a science experiment. If the activities of today have completely drained you, try and pinpoint something you find particularly taxing and change it. For example, if your daily commute is stressful and long, ask if you can work from home for the day and see how that changes your perspective. While it may not be easy to face the facts that your routine is not serving you, making changes where there are red flags will ultimately bring you a happier life.

To be quite honest, constant mindfulness can be exhausting. Your brain only has so much capacity to function at its highest level before it needs a break. If you feel you do your best thinking in the morning, try starting more mindfulness training as you wake up and get ready for your day. Be sure to recognize mental fatigue and take a break. Sometimes doing a mindless task, like entering numbers into a computer, can be a nice vacation for your brain. Once you are recharged, begin your mindfulness again. On top of that, be sure to get a good night's sleep, as uninterrupted as possible, to prepare your brain for another day of mindfulness.

CHAPTER 8:
Train Your Brain for Positive Thoughts

The laws of energy are a very well-known force of nature. We know that when we emit positive energy, we are likely to receive positive energy back. Emitting positive energy isn't just what we put out there, it is what we think internally.

First, let's begin with what we say, and our actions. We have all come across a person or two in life who always says negative things, and finds a way to find the bad in all of the good. What do you think of that person? If you were to see their aura, would it be a positive or negative light? Would they have any glow at all?

Does that same person tend to have bad things happen to them? Is their luck a little lacking? It is really no wonder, as they are attracting negative energies toward themselves. On the other hand, if you look at  what positive people tend to attract their way, we can see that creating positivity around you brings about good energy and good karma.

Is it possible to change the course of our lives for the better just by thinking positively? Absolutely! What we have learned is that thinking positively not only attracts good things to you, it retrains your brain to think in a very optimistic way. On a personal level, it is easier to accomplish tasks and meet goals if you think positively.

For example, if your goal is to finish college and build a career, having a negative attitude about it will certainly hinder your progress, and possibly even hold you back from getting started. You likely talk yourself out of even applying to colleges, for fear and certainty that you will not be accepted.

This fear and negativity will hold you back from having the life you want to lead. Replacing that negativity with positive thoughts builds your confidence, enforcing the fact that you can do whatever it is you want to do, provided you put in a valiant effort.

Take a break from reading for a few minutes. Simply monitor the thoughts running through your head for about ten minutes. Take stock of how many thoughts are pure and positive, and how many are uncertain, negative or pessimistic. What exactly is this getting you? With thousands of thoughts running through your head daily, this adds up to a lot of wasted negative energy.

Now is the time to retrain your brain to think positive. The brain is an amazing organ, sucking up information and analyzing it starting with the very first breath we take. On a physical level, the brain accepts signals from your eyes, ears and other sense organs. The brain processes it as quickly as possible to make sense of it.

Once a decision is made, a pathway of neurons from signal to understanding is created. Once this signal is seen again, it can be processed very quickly to this inevitable understanding. Think about touching your hand to a hot stove. You will develop a pathway to understanding that touching it leads to pain, something you will not do again.

While this has its obvious benefits with physical danger, it doesn't play out so well for other aspects of life. For example, perhaps that perceived danger is you being rejected by a possible boyfriend or girlfriend. The negative experience teaches you not to take chances and talk to potential mates for the fear of future rejection. This hinders the progress of your life.

The good news is, new pathways can be built to replace old ones. All it takes is mindfulness of your thoughts and the ability to actively reroute those thoughts to positive outcomes. This process will take an investment in time, but the end result will certainly be worth it. Start with these simple steps and think up a more positive life for yourself.

Monitor your thoughts every day: Commit yourself to at least ten minutes per day of thought monitoring. Take some time to write your thoughts down simply for what they are.

Rework your thoughts: When you have a negative thought, focus on it, and actively turn it around. For example, when you are stuck in traffic, you may think that you will never make it work on time, and you will surely have a bad day because of it. Instead, ask yourself what you can do to improve this situation. Can you call work and let them know? Would this ease the tension? Even if it doesn't, the situation is what it is, so you might as well enjoy it. Take a look at the scenery around you, listen to your favorite music and take the time to relax. It is what you make of it.

Start your day with a positive thought: If the negativity tends to begin with the sound of your alarm clock, this sets the tone for the rest of the day. Before getting out of bed, flip on the light, take in the room around you and come up with something positive to look forward to  today. Think about what you are thankful for, what fun activity you have planned for today, anything to start the day off right.

CHAPTER 9:
Awaken Your Inner Self with Guided Meditation (1000): Wisdom and Clarity Received From Your Divine Self.

Meditation is a great way to become more mindful of your thoughts and to get in touch with your inner self. Doing so brings you the clarity of mind to determine what it is you want out of life. In this fast-paced world, we often forget to check in with our true desires in exchange for meeting deadlines and catering to others.

A simple practice of meditation every day can get you back in touch with your mind, opening doors and possibilities all around you. Getting started with meditation is easy. It does not require any fancy equipment or atmosphere. All you need is a quiet space, a willing mind and a little bit of time.

There are many different types of meditation, so finding something that speaks to you will be the goal. There is no right or wrong way to do it, so long as you feel refreshed and renewed with the practice. If you are new to meditation, it may help to have a few guided sessions to get a feel for it.

The idea is very simple, and can easily be done on your own. Find a quiet, comfortable room. Find a comfy chair or sit upright on your bed. Avoid laying down, as you may simply fall asleep. Dim the lights if possible and remove any distractions. Leave your cell phone and computer in another room.

Start breathing in and out, slowly and steadily, focusing on the sound of your breath. Put your energy into listening intently on this sound, and don't let your mind wander to other things. Just be at the moment. If it helps, using a guided meditation soundtrack or chanting can help focus the thought. Sometimes focusing on the breath actually quickens it, which isn't what we want.

This is really it. The goal is to relax your brain, giving it a break from the tireless thoughts of the day. You should feel relaxed and refreshed, ready to think fresh, positive thoughts for the rest of the day. With practice, it will become easier to get yourself to this state.

For more advanced practice, and to focus in on your inner self and your true desires, guided thought meditation can certainly help. Use the meditation time more actively and ask yourself to imagine what it is you want your life to look like. Ask your mind to conjure up a detailed image of what that looks like. Ask for clarity and guidance to reach those goals.

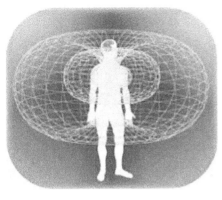 This may not come easily, so don't become frustrated. If it has been a long time since you have listened to your inner self, it may be difficult to get in touch and really know what you want. With practice, those details will begin to emerge. Stay true to your practice every day, and soon you will be able to envision what it is you really need.

With meditation, you can also maneuver through your energy field. Once you get to a good state, begin to imagine that your body is a magnet, and envision the world around you as an infinite energy field. Everything around you gives energy. Look outside to see the trees and grass, the sky and the clouds. It all emits energy, look at it vibrating. Now imagine all of that energy drawing toward you, entering your body through the very crown of your head.

Feel it encircle your entire body. It enters from above but quickly engulfs your belly area, swirling around all of your organs, and soon finding its way to each finger and toe. It courses  through you, invigorating every cell. Feel it wash every negative thought from your mind, and replace it with purity and positivity.

Keep in mind that because energy is constantly moving and changing, you cannot expect your meditation to remain constant. Changing your technique and following your inner needs will help ensure that you are getting the most from your practice.

In case you need more reasons besides inner peace to practice meditation, studies show that regular meditation improves mental stability, improves concentration and productivity, enhances relationships and supports good physical health as well. It lowers stress, therefore reducing blood pressure and heart disease. The benefits are outstanding for such a simple practice. Why not get started today? Right now?

CHAPTER 10:
Awaken Your Intuition

Our natural intuition is what helps guide our decision making. It is the gut feeling we get when something doesn't feel quite right. The decisions made by intuition don't always make rational sense to the brain, but that is because we are listening to our inner wisdom, which has a broader scope of information to go on. Your intuition is something that has always been with you and continues to try and catch your attention, but you are not listening.

You may be out of touch with your intuition if you are feeling generally unguided. You may feel as if even small decisions are difficult to make, and those decisions may lead you down a path that does not suit your best interests. If this sounds like the course of your life right now, it is time to get back on track by tapping into your natural intuition.

Being more mindful of your thoughts and subtle feelings throughout the day is a great way to get in touch with your intuition. We often ignore feelings of discomfort or dissatisfaction for the  perceived greater good. We continue to go to jobs we don't really like for the sake of affording the bills. We continue to see specific friends even though they don't bring out our best selves. It is often easier to carry out these comfortable tasks to make things easier, as change can be difficult.

Now is the time to embrace the idea of bigger and better things. Are you truly happy with your job? Your circle of friends? Do you like the way you feel waking up in the morning, or do you feel unhealthy? Being honest with yourself will help make those tough decisions much easier. Stop burying those intuitive feelings and let them bubble to the surface.

If you aren't sure exactly how to simply 'listen' to yourself, try doing more creative things to get the juices flowing. This could be anything from keeping a journal of your thoughts and feelings, to various types of art. It could be gardening and connecting more deeply with nature, or simply being more attentive to your thoughts.

Being creative is an activity of the spirit. When we do things like balancing the checkbook or do household chores, there is already a basic template for how it should be done. The framework for these tasks is always the same and doesn't allow any opportunity for the brain to stretch beyond its current capacity. However, creating something out of nothing is an exercise, something that requires inner strength, confidence, and guidance.

If you have ever written a book or created a piece of art, you may understand this feeling. Beyond the physical act of typing away at your keyboard or applying paint to a canvas, you actually go into a sort-of trance as you work. Your analytical brain takes a break, and your creative brain goes on autopilot. The result is a piece of work that has come directly from your inner spirit, something your analytical brain could have never imagined.

Once you find something creative that you love, let your spirit take off. Do whatever it is your spirit compels you to do. Experiment with new types of paints, try clay, take a hike in a new area, whatever the case may be. Learning to follow this intuition in a controlled environment actually trains you to let intuition take over when it really counts. As you practice these skills, you will realize that they have the same application in everyday life.

Your job can be run the same way. Allow some creativity to hold your interest, and if your intuition is leaving you blank, maybe it is time to make a shift in your life. Asking for new assignments that compel your creativity and intuition become your new art, and success is sure to follow. Remaining stagnant and following the same pattern does not allow that intuition to grow and change, which it will naturally want to do.

No matter how you choose to listen, harness the power of your intuition and don't be afraid to follow it. The biggest mistake you can make is hearing your intuition and squashing its power by not making any necessary changes. Life is all about flow and change. Staying stagnant and refusing to make important decisions do not keep us in good pace with the energy of the universe. Learning to fully function with intuition as our guide will ensure we are abreast of all of the positive things that may come our way.

CHAPTER 11:
Reduce Stress with Guided Meditation

What are the biggest causes of your stress? Most people would say that daily stressors, like family and jobs, are the main reason they lose sleep at night. While we certainly can't choose to remove all of these stresses from life, we can certainly learn to manage them better.

The main reason stress creates such havoc on the mind and body is because it distracts us from our true purposes in life. It is hard to contemplate the meaning of life and explore your spirit if you are bogged down in traffic jams and paperwork. If your day is filled with a litany of mindless tasks, stress will surely get to you.

Stress is a necessary part of life. The adrenaline rush and hormone push associated with stress create a sense of urgency that helps us get things done. It is both a blessing and a curse. From a physiological perspective, stress is a built-in process that began with early man. It was meant to raise blood pressure, heart rate and provide adrenaline to muscles to avoid danger.

These days, there aren't as many physical dangers for us to run from, but rather emotional stress has taken its place. If you were to literally run from your problems, the hormone response would cease, and the body could return to normal. Unfortunately, there isn't much physical about conquering your problems.

Instead, this low-level amount of stress causes hormones to stay out of whack, causing problems all around the body when it comes to health. That increase in heart rate and blood pressure turn into chronic hypertension and heart disease. Other hormones cause weight gain and fatigue. Stress on our bodies creates stress on our mind as well. Lots of energy will go to these areas to try and compensate, leaving the mind and spirit sucked dry.

It is time to get that energy back by destressing our lives. The first step is to eliminate any unnecessary stress. Perhaps you tend to take on too many projects at once. Regulating how much you take on is a great first step. Don't volunteer to drive carpool if you already have a doctors' appointment, important work presentation, and dinner to make, all in one day. Begin to recognize your threshold for stress and stay within it.

Often, the company we keep is a great source of stress. We all have friends that tend to suck all of our energy. Their problems become our problems, and you end up stuck dealing with it. While it is great to help people out, doing so by sacrificing your own well-being is not the way to do it. Feel free to set stricter boundaries to protect your inner spirit from becoming bogged down.

Of course, meditation will play a big role in stress relief as well.

As we mentioned in earlier chapters, the idea of meditation is to refocus the mind and allow only simple thoughts at any given time. Living in the current moment and shutting down all thought gives the mind and spirit a rest. Think of it the same as sleep for your body. With proper rest, the mind and spirit can begin again anew, more ready than ever to tackle problems.

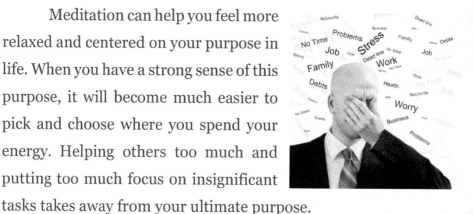

Meditation can help you feel more relaxed and centered on your purpose in life. When you have a strong sense of this purpose, it will become much easier to pick and choose where you spend your energy. Helping others too much and putting too much focus on insignificant tasks takes away from your ultimate purpose.

Using methods of guided meditation with experienced teachers can be a great way to open the mind and find your focus again. While traditional meditation on your own will certainly have its benefits, using a recorded session or an in-person visit with a meditation expert can help you open up to new possibilities and ways of thinking.

For example, if you are stressed in a professional manner, and feel like you are misguided, guided meditation that focuses the mind on your career goals can be most beneficial. An expert may ask you to imagine different scenarios in relation to your job, and how your overall career goal fits into your ideal lifestyle. Finding disconnections between these two areas of your life can help you re-evaluate your path.

Let's say your current career is in finance, as you have a love for numbers. However, this career has led you to approving and denying loans for people. Maybe this aspect of the job goes against your moral values, and it actually makes your spirit dim to carry out this task. This realization could lead to a powerful shift in your career to better align with your values.

As you go about this type of meditation, it is important to keep an open mind to the possibilities. Discovering the truth and deciding not to do anything to change your circumstances will quickly wear your inner spirit. Be optimistic and open to taking a new route in life to better flow with your energy.

CHAPTER 12:
Create a Stronger Brain with Meditation

To this point, the benefits of meditation have been relatively intangible. Effects of stress and wellbeing are felt differently by each person, and therefore, isn't measurable in a scientific sense.

However, we can measure overall brain function and structure change relative to meditation. It has been done, and the results are striking. Landmark studies have shown that with as little as six weeks of new meditation practice can have a lasting effect on the brain.

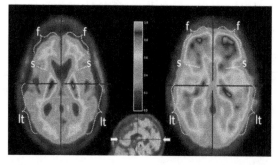

First and foremost, the amygdala, the area responsible for causing feelings of anxiety and stress was shown to shrink with meditation. In addition, areas of the brain that flourish in compassion and creative thought grow exponentially. Brain scans show that people who meditate have bigger areas of gray matter and that more of it is used at any given time.

This means that your brain is working as a whole to be analytical, compassionate and creative when dealing with problems, as opposed to being closed minded and only seeing things from one side. Any good problem solver knows that there is never just one solution, and the real trick is choosing the best answer from a list of possibilities. Creating those possibilities is all about imagination and brain power.

We certainly cannot underestimate the power of brain exercise. We need to treat the brain the same as any muscle in the body. With exercise and conditioning, muscles grow larger and more capable of tasks. This is also true with the brain.

It is not far-fetched, then, to assume that regular exercise for our brain will improve our memory, reduce stress and create an overall better sense of self. Luckily, science is on our side with this.

Lots of methods are known to increase brain power, including games testing analytical ability and memory. Perhaps more compelling, however, are methods that increase our senses of humanity. Enhancing our ability to understand our needs, and those of others, to feel compassion and empathy for others are skills this world certainly needs more of.

Creative thought and meditation are the best ways to enhance these areas of the brain. Stress relief seems to be the key to allow this. As we described earlier, stress taxes the brain, making it difficult to think and focus on anything but the stressor at hand. With meditation, that stress is reduced, allowing more energy for productive thought.

A more capable brain can make better sense of new stresses and situations, seeing them from a higher perspective. Being above a situation instead of entrenched in it makes it easier to see a way out.

Imagine that in times of stress, you are deep in a dark forest, unable to see the way out. When your mind is clear and focused, you are instead visualizing the problem from the top of the tallest tree. In the distance, you see the way. The way to eliminate stress is to have a confident direction and plan, something that can be achieved through meditation.

CHAPTER 13:
5-Minute Guided Meditation

This quick five-minute guided meditation session is meant to calm your body and mind quickly during times of stress. This mini-session is great to keep at work or in other stressful environment where time is of the essence.

Stress builds up quickly throughout the day, and it is necessary to take small breaks to realign your purpose and focus your attention back on the task at hand. Consider this five minutes time to file away all of your thoughts and prepare your mind with a clean slate, ready to face the rest of your day.

Use this meditation session anytime you need a break, are feeling sluggish and drained, or just when you feel like closing your eyes and escaping your racing thoughts. Simply find a quiet room or space, dim the lights if possible, and sit comfortably. Enjoy!

Begin by taking a seated or lying down position. Settle in to your spot and get comfortable. Sit so there is equal pressure on your buttocks, and so the vertebrae in your spine are in a straight alignment. Release the pressure on your problem areas and allow the entirety of your body to share the task of carrying your weight. Together, all of your muscles, bones, and tendons are strong, and as one, can accomplish anything.

Gently close your eyes. Take a deep breath, slowly in, then slowly back out.

On your next breath, pull in just a little more air than the breath before. Exhale slowly, steadily, pushing every last bit of air out with it. Push it out with your abdominal muscles.

Imagine that each breath in is the acceptance of positive energy from the universe. Feel it flowing through you, so tangible that you can see the little flecks of silver and gold light as they rush to enter your body. Feel it course through your entire body. It begins in your lungs but quickly rushes through your blood, reaching every cell in every part of your body. Feel the excited energy flow to your fingers and toes, barely held there, bursting with life.

As you exhale, imagine that your body has gathered up all of your negative thoughts, emotions, and energy on that inhale, and is now expressing it back into the universe. It is there that the highest of energy will neutralize that negativity and bring balance. Push that breath out, seeing the red flecks of negativity swirling outward. You are free of it.

Now, focus all of your attention solely on your own body and spirit. As you sit, still and comfortable, feel the existence of the top of your head. It is your closest connection to the higher universe. Feel the energy coursing in and out. Feel it travel down your spine, energizing every vertebra on the way down.

Feel that energy, never dulling, rushing down your abdomen, encircling all of your inner organs, revitalizing your cells and breathing life into your core. There is so much that the excess quickly travels down your arm, your legs, and brings rejuvenation to your tired, achy muscles. Feel the warmth as you accept this energy.

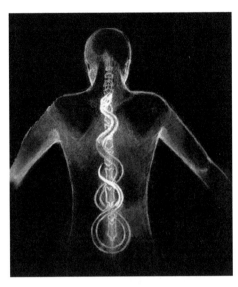

Continue breathing slowly, in and out, at a pace that is comfortable for your body. With each breath, slow the pattern, breathing in slower, exhaling lightly, but entirely. Feel your inhale catch after a moment of complete still at the end of your exhale. That is your calm.

At that moment, your body rests, poised and ready to inhale the breath of a new day, a new adventure. With this breath, accept all that is good in this world, and set forth a new attitude and mindset to carry the rest of your day. Breathe positivity and joy into everything that you do.

You are capable, strong, energized and positive. There is nothing on this worldly planet that could bring you down. Go forth renewed, refreshed and ready to conquer your day.

CHAPTER 14:
30-Minute Guided Meditation (1000)

This guided meditation session is designed to put your mind and body in a state of euphoria, one that opens your mind and clears it of unnecessary stress. Practicing meditation on a daily basis reduces overall stress, increases your problem-solving abilities and connects you with your inner self, your guide to living your best life.

To begin, find a quiet spot to sit, relaxed and comfortable. Make sure the room is at a good, warm temperature so that you feel completely relaxed. The goal is to find a space where you are not distracted by outside noise or discomfort, and you can focus fully on your meditation practice.

Begin by closing your eyes slowly. See the world dim as you do so. Take a deep breath in, completely filling your lungs, then exhale slowly and deliberately, to completion.

Continue breathing, focusing your attention only on the sound of the breath. Imagine that each breath in and out creates the same sound as waves gently meeting the beach. Each wave brings in a new energy, with the power to wash away the small pebbles away when

it leaves. Imagine that each breath you exhale is the wave pulling your negative energy back into the ocean.

Hear the waves bubble and crackle. Look down the beach, only to see an endless stretch of sand, light, and tan, starkly contrasting the dark blue sea. Expand your view to see both land and sea contrast with the blue sky. There is nothing else here, no people, no problems, no worry.

Feel the waves lap up against your feet, slowly burying your feet in the sand. Feel the coarse pebbles against the soles of your feet. Feel it tickle as each wave pulls those pebbles out from under your feet.

Watch the water swirl around your ankles, unphased by their presence. The water continues to use its energy to fill every space.

With your next breath, smell the salt of the sea fill your nasal passages, sharp and crisp. Feel the warm air blow gently against your face. The sun beats down, warming your skin.

In this reverie, close your eyes. The sight of the beach disappears into nothing, and all that is left is the sound of the ocean crashing against the beach. All you feel is the warmth of the sun on your face and shoulders, warming you to your very core.

Open your eyes now to see a field of daisies, spread out infinitely around you. You look to the horizon to see yellow and white specs spread throughout the green of the leaves. The sun shines down, illuminating the glow of the daisy petals on the flowers within arms' reach.

You inspect the petals, eyeing their delicate curves, how they meet the center of the flower in a very symmetrical, orderly fashion. Your eye is caught by the center and gets entangled in the spiral that is the center. The intricacy is fascinating and perfect.

The sound of birds chirping enters your reverie. You begin to see them flitting back and forth overhead, dancing with each other. You appreciate their boundless energy, driven by nothing but their playful relationships with each other. They simply play, with no other care in the world.

As you sit in silence, you recognize the magnitude of life hidden within this field. The flowers seem endless. As you look closer, you begin to see the busy movement of honey bees, little specs visiting each flower, staying only for a moment. It is all moving, all constantly moving. This compels you to action, but only for a fleeting moment.

You are energized and refreshed witnessing these tiny beings carry out their work. You begin to feel a warm energy building within your chest, an excited feeling. You feel relaxed, renewed and ready to stand, walk, run.

This day is yours. It is your time to use your powerful brain, to listen to your inner spirit, to be driven by your intuition. Within you holds all of the wisdom and power you could ever need. Go forth knowing that your spirit is all-knowing and your path will be revealed, if you are willing to accept it.

Open your eyes. Take a final deep breath in and out. As you breathe in, accept all of the good energy the universe has to provide you. As you exhale, gather all of the stress and negative energy within you and expel it with a powerful force. Feel that energy deep within your chest starts to rise again. Feel the excitement that fills your spirit.

You are now ready to begin again, renewed and refreshed. Open your eyes, gather your presence back in this world. Feel the energy rush through every inch of you, fingers and toes. Follow your spirit and accepts its wisdom.

This ends the guided meditation session. Use this imagery as often as necessary to enhance your mood, gather your positive energy and tackle the day. Go forth in peace.

Conclusion

Thank you for making it through to the end of *Third Eye Awakening for Beginners: 10 Steps to Activate and Decalcify Your Pineal Gland, Open the Third Eye Chakra, and Increase Mind Power through Guided Meditation*. Let's hope it was informative and able to provide you with all of the tools you need to achieve your goals of creating a better life for yourself.

Having read this book, you should have a better understanding of your place in the universe. You know that the energies within you interact with that of the universe. Everything you do creates energy and choosing to emit positivity and light give you the same in return.

You are now equipped with the meditation tools necessary to shape your daily life. Meditation and mindfulness are the keys to becoming more in tune with your energy and your personal needs. Practice this daily to be present in your life.

The next step is to harness the knowledge inside this book and use it to create the life you have always dreamed about. Anything is possible if you utilize the energy flow of the universe.

Finally, if you found this book useful in any way, a review on Amazon is always appreciated!

Description

For ages, humans have pondered the meaning of life, and their purpose here on this Earth. While no single answer to this question exists, we do know that we are each individually connected to the energies of the universe.

The state of our lives is highly dependent on how we utilize that energy, and how well we understand our inner selves and our connection to the bigger picture. Becoming more enlightened and aware of our place in the universe, the alignment of our individual energy and the careful emission of positive energy into the system is responsible for our wellness outcomes.

Learning how our individual energy works and making adjustments where necessary can make exponentially great changes in the trajectory of our existence. A life full of stress, misfortune, and bad luck can quickly be relieved by listening to your inner self, the intuition, the third eye, within you. Learn to harness the power within to make positive changes to your circumstances. This requires a great deal of focus, mental prowess, and commitment, but it can be done.

Now is a great time to live the life you have always wanted. This will be achieved through the mental and physical adjustments outlined in this book. Don't wait to receive energy from the universe, it is yours for the taking.

www.ingramcontent.com/pod-product-compliance
Lightning Source LLC
LaVergne TN
LVHW020905240425
809281LV00021B/17